HERD QUEEN

Di Slaney is a poet, publisher and animal sanctuary founder who lives in Nottinghamshire. She has an MA in Creative Writing from Nottingham Trent University and owns Candlestick Press (famed for 'poetry pamphlets, instead of a card'). Her poems have been published in various magazines including *Magma*, *The Rialto*, *The Interpreter's House* and *Brittle Star*, and twice shortlisted for the Bridport Prize. Her debut pamphlet *Dad's Slideshow* was published by Stonewood Press in 2015.

In 2005, Di and her husband moved into a Grade II Listed four-hundred-year-old farmhouse, populating it with livestock and eventually starting Manor Farm Charitable Trust. The house, the animals, and the surrounding village of Bilsthorpe became the subjects of her first full-length collection of poetry, *Reward for Winter*, published by Valley Press in 2016.

Herd Queen

DI SLANEY

Valley Press

First published in 2020 by Valley Press
Woodend, The Crescent, Scarborough, YO11 2PW
www.valleypressuk.com

ISBN 978-1-912436-41-5
Cat. no. VP0161

A CIP record for this book is available from the British Library.

Cover photograph by Di Slaney.
Cover and text design by Jamie McGarry.
Edited by Jo Haywood.

Printed and bound in Great Britain by
Imprint Digital, Upton Pyne, Exeter.

Contents

PART THREE: A HEX FOR MODERN TIMES

In memory of Billy (2002 – 2019)
under whose watchful gaze and gentle snores
all these poems were written.

PART ONE

Rosemary thrives

Talking donkey

Says *friendship* is grooming
      His teeth to mane, mouth on cross
Says *sadness* is going,
      Her softbreath kiss, gateclick-gateclick
Says *patience* is watching
      Hours stand in grass and clouds
Says *straw* is sunlight
      He chews summer, tongues tractor
Says *bucket* is mirror
      His nose in blackwet
Says *happy* is rolling
      Hot dust rises, hooves flail
Says *hungry* is apples
      Hand in pocket, first bite
Says *strength* is bray
      He dredges his chest
Says *truth* is warm
      How it wraps like his mother's neck
Says *silence* never is
      His ears catch every spiderspin

Meeting Geraldine

'Big goat left to die in snow' was all that I
was told, and that she was old, so promised
I would go along to meet her, see how her
ordeal had left her and if there were no
major complications, nothing more
they could do, I'd bring her here. Fear

penned her nosefirst in that stable corner, fear
so strong the reek of it sank me to my knees. I
softtouched her coat and bones, promised
I would do the best I could, would give her
all the food she needed to be well. She made no
sound, didn't move or flinch, had more

sorespots than I'd first noticed, more
dirt than grey in thinwhitecoat. The fear
kept her silent that first week when all I
did was strawsit with her, promising
she could have a friend, that her
hollowrumen hungeraches would end, no

one would hurt her here. There was no
clue she'd heard or understood, it was more
that she put up with me. Yearslearnt fear
still flickered in her eyes each time I
tugged the stable door, the promise
I'd be back offering no comfort, her

nostrils alarmwide with whiff of me. But her
appetite was good and she had no
trouble eating, brokenmouthed with more
teeth missing than remained. One day, fear
seemed to hover above the haypile and I
breathstopped while she cudded, promising

myself patience would pay, promising
her the moon if only she'd respond. Then her
blackovals set in gold met startledmine, no
hesitation now with ears uppricked, more
curious with nose cleanpink and wet. Fear
evaporated like milkspurt on warm grass and I

kept my word every day after, although we only had
her for a year. She died in May whitesunshine while
I stroked her beard, promised her no more fear.

Herd Queen

I wouldn't be in this mess if I was a goat.
I'd be queen of the hill, grumpiest nanny,
up her arse with my horns every false step,
catching her knees with a serrated smack
when she least expects it. I'd swerve as she
reached to shove me away, and if she tried
to gain the higher ground, I'd dance ahead
so fast she'd puff and chuff for nothing, my
deep bleats rolling down the valley to scorn
her feebles. She could preen and prance
as much as she liked; my coat thicker,
hooves harder, my teeth more inclined
to nip. She'd misread my wagging tail,
ignore my red pulsating rear and soft rank
whiff of rut, my curling flehmen lip. She'd
lean in, get up so close my hot backfired cud
lands in her open maw, then one swift butt
splits her nose with a crack, like a sniper's shot.

In every group of goats, a 'herd queen' will emerge to lead the
way. She has earned her place at the top of the hierarchy by
proving her strength and stamina in battle with other does,
sometimes with bucks too. The herd queen is the leader for
life, and gets the best sleeping spot, first dibs at the food, the
tastiest plants and treats. She influences all decisions, protects
and defends against all comers, and although she may lose her
supremacy in old age, will always retain the respect of the herd.

Jubilate Excreta

For it is an excellent indicator of overall wellbeing
For we have rather a lot of it, out on the field
For I am the servant of all of these pooping animals
For there are many and several varieties
For the foremost of these is ovine
For there are five sub-categories of ovine
For fifthly there is the splat which looks as it sounds
For fourthly there is the mousse, which once pictured is hard to
    ignore when eating a chocolate one
For thirdly there is the sausage, and the likelihood of worms
    For those worms may be tape or round or barberpole or lung or
        liver fluke
    For the sheep may die from these worms unless dosed with an
        appropriate wormer
    For prevention is better than cure
    For garlic helps in their diet
    For diatomaceous earth also helps in their diet
    For regular paddock rotation reduces the number of infective
        larvae on pasture
For secondly there are bunches of grapes
For firstly there are raisins, blessed sign and all hail
For when it floats to the surface after heavy rain, it is easier to collect
For it helps to weigh down the composter to compact the straw
For if we had time to use it, it would be excellent garden mulch
For it helps to fill rabbit holes to stop the animals breaking their legs
For it smells like molasses and grass and sweetlicksickness
For it smells better than regurgitated cud belched in your face
For it sticks to fleece like glue and won't be easily wiped off
    For it attracts the flies in summer
    For those flies lay their eggs in it
    For those eggs become maggots
    For those maggots eat the sheep alive
    For the sheep will die
    For the sheep must be sprayed with CLiK to keep the flies away
    For this is our uppermost dread

For when we find the maggots we must pick out every single one
For this can take hours
For if we miss one maggot the sheep may die
For poo must be solid and never liquid
For we talk about it all the time
For it is one of the four main things in life
For food, water and shelter are the other three
For it glistens in the sunshine
For it hardens in winter
For it trickles into your welly when you push the wheelbarrow uphill
For it squidges underfoot
For it sticks like clay in the ridges of your sole
For you will tiptoe through the house in your wellies to avoid
    shedding it on the tiles
For when you fall in it you will always find the biggest pile

Doggebrikke

They caught me when I lurched across the brickyard in the sun, blinking lightdazzled after all that chewchain barntime, my name a muttered lipcurse, my jaws a drooling fooltrap, my claws the devil's slashspite, or so they claimed. The stink of blackfear hovered like thunderburst above their heads, reeking pissshit malice, hands pulling and dragging and poking so the print I left in the settingbrick dug deep and slant. The child saved it for memory, my paw behind the door in this halfbuilt farmwall the last I saw before redblack, redblack, red, red. Black.

Mazey ball

She watched him gather tufts from fences
along the field, as he'd watched her finger wool
in the village yarn shop, her gaze low and dark, small
brown hands lingering over skeins still fresh
from early shearing. That night he switched off all
the lights and kept squat candles burning on the hearth,

their flicker pointing beams and cracks in ancient brickwork.
His thickweave cushions, driftwood hangings and peg
loom rugs brought the flock indoors, while by the fire
raw fleece sacks breathed their sweetness across
the room towards the porch. Single storeyed, the cottage
eased itself to darkness as he doused his mug goodnight

and padded to the bed, cablesocks three quarters high
on tanned and knotted calves, tired legs. The ball twined
above the kitchen stove where a skillet used to drop,
anchored by aran ply to a thumbed black squab.
Candlelight caught cream, a flash of white, then grey
as the ball twisted first this way, then that. He lay on one

hundred quilted crochet squares, felt each deadwifestitch
pressing into skin like penance, but resolute he still listened;
breathsure, heartloose. When the front latch snagged at two,
he smiled and reached beneath the bed, shepherded silence
along the flags to find her backwards in the shadows, ball in hand,
bloodblack hair flowing down a feltstiff gown above her knees.

Skin glistened, and she seemed to halo pale fawn fibre
that curled towards him, her bare feet pointed in two cleaves
of hoof, and soft noise escaped her lips like new lambs bleating
in barn sunlight. She never shifted from the ball, kept
mumblecounting little threads, so he gently snaked his crook
around her neck like every ewe he'd ever landed, and snared his witch.

Mayhem the Herdwick

is nothing like his name. He holds proud,
close but not against, calm but not without
action, shortbreaths huffing to cloud
your view of a skyline as grey as doubt
on this slow October day. Allowed
to take a biscuit, bristlehairy nose pokes
your pocket for more, while wetfleece
damps your leg. His top layer smoky
guardhairs evoke carpets, footstools, creased
up wiry cushions too coarse for heads. Broken
hoof walls beg a foot trim, a chance to wrestle
woolbulk and gulp this fragrant heap
whose persistent lanolin gloryrises to nest
your nostrils. All day you will smell sheep.

Driving to Much Wenlock

Heady, this rich waft of lanolin blowing
through the grill, the Jeep packed with ripe
fleeces from Friday's shearing. I'm showing
flesh today with shirt sleeves rolled, wipe

a tickle of sweat from my top lip, a prick
of wrigglewarm under my skin, and turn up
the radio for 'Sunshine on Leith' as heat licks
the dash. I squint. April pulses like a randy tup

in all the lush fields flashing by the window
so I roll it down, the smell of pee and clags
rising in my nostrils with flickerburn to run. I go
faster, see all the weight of wool behind, dags

poking through netstrings with their reek
of shit and earth, see without mirror, see back
and sides without moving head, feel sleek
cream locks creeping from behind to meet black

tufts on me, one long wrap of grey and downy
thel to swathe me as the sky and road merge
and I baabreathe through my mouth, baabrown
cudjuice leaking from my lips and oh, that surge

of powerjoy to leap from this box and jump, jump, jump
away into the green

Rosemary thrives

'…where the mistress is master.' Old English garden lore

She snips green sprigs at midnight while
he snores, those small black scissors snug
in her apron pouch all day, waiting. Styling
long woody stems through her hair, she tugs
and drags the needles against her mind,
raking a tang of sea to recall a better lot.
She hums as she weaves, the leaves an unkind
spiky wreath to prick her forehead but not
one whit of regret. She chews, and savours each
sharp twist and roll, adds more to the pot and brews
a pale gold tea so finely scented, he'll down and reach
for more, his narrowed heart beating too fast will lose
its measured rhythm, upend itself, run aground.

Abele

'White poplar was widely thought to be non-native, however, references to "abel" trees in historic documents indicate it has been here much longer than previously thought.' Woodland Trust

I want to be composted here when I die,
somewhere between the white poplars in my
own Elysian field. Years of sweat will turn my hair
the colour of their leaves like Hercules escaping the lair
of Cacus. A cardboard coffin will do, but please
don't burn me; I want to rot down slowly, tease
the worms and beetles with my juices, tempt
sucking roots to wriggle over my straying, unkempt
bones. You can tuck some keepsakes in beside me,
a few idle things to while away the time. Three
at most, there must be room for my dishevelled skin
to drop and slough away. Then when it's time to begin
again without me, don't cry. When you see
Diana in the sky, milky opals gleaming on the hill, be
glad I'm home forever at the base of such a tree.

The green wood sculptor at Gabriel's Wharf

'Cutting into wood means shaping solidified time.' Friedel Buecking

The first time I saw his work, it was two
weeks after that sudden bloody death and
three days before I'd sit stroking her head
as breath slowed minutes, shaped hours.

In between, his playful rugged pieces a delight
against all that glass, those many angles, so much
straight. His firm nicks and creases snagpulled
my palm, some urgent city warmth still rising

through grain from the weekday's hardboiled
sun. I pressed my cheek to one tall totem, heard
office secrets sniggered through the chainsaw's
roar, tipsy chatter marking wooden ears but

not the man himself; too short to be an angel,
too roughhewn canny to live anywhere here.

Belly pot

A man should have bought this one, not me.
He would relish the gorgeous swell
from neck to base, the upturned bell
with smooth, cool lip and open pout. He

would be helpless, unable to resist the trail
of icing glaze glistening over warm red spice,
fondant on coarse ginger, want to cut a slice
and touch it with his tongue, taste earth. Braille

pimples every coil with dimples underneath,
her secret imprint hard to spot, this time no
colour marker paints it out. He would go
to the window, heft it to the light, breath

catching at the weight, turn it slowly, linger
as sun scorches it to umber, find her finger.

Please touch

You'd shoved this one to the back of the shelf, but
I liked her. Something about her rough edges,
uneven profile broken but strong, dollops and wedges
of chocolate against blushing white. Humming to
myself, I picked her up and traced her crags from
                    front to back, round and down,
                    up and under.
Your pencilled tag was faded, she'd been here
a while. Twenty pounds nothing at all, in the price
of things. And I felt jaded too, pissed off at
being ignored yet still wanting to be worthy.
She felt good in hand, started to warm to my touch,
much softer despite some jagged bits. I loved
those earthy colours, knew she would look good
next to the bed, stark lines shadowed on the
curtains. Yes, she was ready to come home with
                    me, take up her spot. Hold me steady.

Bareback

I don't know which of the farm boys popped
me up there. Mum said the first she knew
was when we came down to the yard, blue
flowers bobbing on brown bareback, cropped

fringe swaying to the soft slow trot
of overgrown hooves, scabby fists tugging
that dark tangled mane. I forgot
my fear in the telling at school, hugging

Mum no part of the story, just how
the ruts and furrows of the plough
nearly unseated me but that strong
old horse worked hard to keep me on,

bring me home. I don't know when he died,
good Robin. I don't remember if I cried.

PTS

Hens always surprise, especially those who seem
already so close to their end, so nearly almost done,
but arch and flap and brace and roll, protest with screams
that she's not leaving yet, no_no_no_no_no_no_____no
when flock goes silent, their many voices shut off by this one.

The sheep slump into it, all fading eyes and rancid
breath, such sad fleecefolds of heaving death,
but then resist with blank solidity the final grace,
jugular evading needle, no blood streaked trace
to speed this passing while you stroke his tired face.

Pony's last moments are too hard, the beauty of her form
lost in incapacity as she drops to ground at the first
and rests head in your lap as the second takes effect,
tears blurring mane to mingle with the fearsweat on her neck.
The donkeys turn to walk away the exact moment she exhales her *ave*.

The goats, for all their singularity, show strength of herd.
Standing vigil, the king appears attentive to each word
meant to soothe the old and broken as she rejects meds
like she fought off new and younger does, butting heads
with it until the dosage proves too strong.
Horns lowered to the fence, the king acknowledges she is gone
and makes sure that the others do the same,
while you unclip the dusty talisman of her name.

Loading the trailer

The photos stopped me scrolling, screen held
up close while my cheeks flushed to match
the colour of her t-shirt, BITCH spelled
out in half-hatched fading letters across

the egg-flat tits drooping to her waist.
The collie at her feet probably was a bitch,
loyal to her click, licking hand to taste
an awful leak of tears that spilled to

soak a farming lifetime's gruffness. Where
her hair was up and pinned, it splayed now
in thin pale strands, forehead shining bare
while October sun picked out scurf

between liver spots and wrinkles. Shrunk
to below the family five-foot marker, behind
the truck and trailer she was lost, too drunk
on memories fully proof of every birth

and death here to admit her own. The last
to leave nuzzled her neck, his giant ears
gently flicking her cheek as he passed
her up the ramp, this one she'd had for

more years than she'd kept a husband, longer
than she'd known a friend. They drove away
while silence wrapped her in its shroud, late
autumn heat unbearable on the yard at midday.

That water

Ignore everything else: the boy, the sun,
our mum, calves on the edge of the bank,
the colour of my jelly shoes shrieking
fun-time red, the rising stinky rank

of cow pats warmed in the heat –
don't think of them leaching into it,
don't think of anything related to shit
at all – put that out of your mind.

Meet me halfway on this – look down
as you see me doing, a little frown
misleading my mood, which is more
happy than sad today – focus like before

with your heart and tongue, eyes tight.
Touch that water, taste calm, hear the clear
and pleasant stranger lapping at your sight,
stroke fronded stones. Breathe out.

Saltfleetby

I am gold and blue and grey,
I am grass and wood and dunes,
I am peat and marsh and salt, licking.

And they say I taste like release, smell
like everything deserved and unbroken.
I make light of their heavy days, give no
quarter on raw, wet mornings when wind blasts
blue, bites down to their bones. Even on black
afternoons when the rain makes them huddle and hop,
nowhere else will do. I am the place they trust to stand buff
and proud, no shame to pack up to take home. What makes them
desperate to arrive makes it difficult to leave. Only the promise they can
come back to my ragged lines and stride out along the sand lets them turn away,
everything laid bare. They say I cut with a blade so sharp, they suck in their cheeks
with my truth, swallow their blood from my blow. No wonder they like it here.
They gain a gentler touch, gloves peel to show hot fingers that ache to feel.

I am gold and blue and grey,
I am grass and wood and dunes,
I am peat and marsh and salt, sticking.

The bridge

And this would be all she
would ever want, although
it would take her forty years
to work it out; years of slow

dark grind and billable hours,
a sine wave of assets won
at a price out of reach for
payment. This faint shower

of rain that upturns her chin
to face the sky, shadows
cutting slices out of trees, thin
layers to buffer summer's breeze

and cushion knees against log
scuffs; all these anchor her to
the earth like a supermarket dog
tied and watching for its owner.

PART TWO

Witness

Stitches

Now you've mentioned it, I can see clearly.
There's wool in every frame. Background
and foreground, on bodies, on shelves – nearly
everyone wearing something knitted. Bound

to be one of her jumpers, because we'd
never be without one, even on the beach.
Look – here we are in June, paddling in the sea,
swimsuits under cardies, sun just out of reach

and wind kept at bay by thick cable striping.
And the black faced sheep in landscape
shots stand boasting their own yarn, hyping
up the baabaabeauty of the fall and drape,

begging us to buy the cones and hanks
stacked in baskets on the floor of craft
shops, alongside fudge gifts for the Yanks.
She would be proud, would have laughed

out loud at all the rollneck turtles on display
on every holiday we had – August, April, May –
with just enough stitches keeping us protected;
too tight to unravel, cast on firm, connected.

Empty pool

after Norman MacCaig

She was set on going in the water,
said her wellies would keep her dry,
promised not to slip. My daughter
had always been the one to try,

to push and rush like reed-tips
in the wind, bending but not breaking.
The way she pursed her lips
and crouched to fish, taking

her chance with that long stick
that reached deep into the brack
made me love her, stoop to pick
up the camera, take a step back

though fears of drowning were
rising like pity in my mind. I couldn't
help if she fell in, can't swim like her
mother who stands watching, wouldn't

leave my guard post by this stone.
I'd keep clicking, follow ripples where she'd gone.

Lucky red

It was a gift, actually, how that
colour grabbed the focus of the frame,
hauled me in. Even that wretched bear
whose name escapes me (she left it everywhere) sat
glowing like a nightlight on her lap. Of course,
the intense phone-and-postbox combination
in the background reinforced all the other sunset
qualities. In such circumstances duplication
can be forgiven, although I'd usually be driven
to retouch or reshoot by the blush of her
cheeks matching that cardigan and fur
exactly. Yes, I suppose they did look sweet
together, all that cradling and smiling for
the lens while rocks made her backside sore.
I didn't notice that, just the crimson wellies on her feet.

West of Dolgellau

I don't know what drives me up
here, to leave them behind
in the gorse and bilberries,
with Marmite, bara brith,
Bourneville and plastic cups
of tea to keep them going.

I always say 'just over the next
hill' and then they tire, give
up and tell me to go on alone,
as they know I always want to,
even though I don't know why
that is. It's not the grey sky

and drizzle, that's for sure;
that's not the lure but there's
something that tugs and pulls
that I'm never able to explain.
When I reach the top, or run
out of steam, or the siling rain

gets too much even for me, then
the urge subsides and I can stop,
shrug off the rucksack, breathe
again. I'm not a man to yearn,
or have ambitions, or want what's
not within my grasp. This burn

inside is soft and slow, a little flame
that won't go out. And so I take my
one shot of the blue and ochre far
below as the sun comes from behind
a cloud, burnishing the quarry water
and turning shale to silver. In the dry

silence after shutter click, I can hear
their voices on the wind, her laughter
carries like a bird riding thermals
through the crags. They feel near
to me up here, closer through the lens
than they will be when I go back down.

Girl with the red hat

If I wasn't a man of few terse
words, I would tell you how
this single frame catches at my
heart, snatches all my gruff and
bombast away, drags me to a past
where we were so very young, your
cherry red hat from my mother
dangling like a lover's swollen
lips from your hand, as if you
knew. Unmanned now, old and
tired, I can feel the same surge,
that heated urge to say or do any
thing to make your laugh sing
out like bells across the sand.

Girl in the bikini

The first time, she uploaded it in colour. Sky
met sea at the light brown gleam of thighs
rising toward a pinker glint of belly, the slight
bow of waist tilting forward, and up higher
blue triangles perked as if they might
fly, have a life of their own which she tried
hard to do, smoked mirrors blanking eyes,
red cap tugged low, long hair straying her disguise.

The second time was in mono, white
and black a perfect binary for his lies,
the shaded aspect of her face curved to fight
what came leftfield while on the right,
sun bleached her slim hand reaching behind
as if the water could turn solid, bolster her reply.

Holding her hand

for Avril Conroy

I wish she had done similar things with me,
made sandcastles and giant earthwork rings with me.

I see my mother and my daughter laughing in the waves,
and taste the salty heartwrench that it wrings from me.

The way she nods holding her hand looks
sweet, yet grates and sourstings on me.

Some gentler words and relaxed rules would
have lifted hopelessheart on wings in me.

I can't remember loving without fear; time
reduced her seldomtouch to nothing to me.

Now I must breach the waves, retrieve
my child as April rescues spring for me.

Witness

Afterwards, she could never remember
how old they both were, that cardboard
sign propped against his breakfast bowl
pushing all thoughts from her head,

PERVERT

they weren't very old, but that cardboard
word bloodred like the raspberry jam
pushed all other thoughts from her head
and his eyes wouldn't meet hers,

PERVERT

cheeks bloodred like the raspberry jam,
his hand shaking, holding the spoon,
and his eyes couldn't meet hers
when she pressed his foot under the table,

PERVERT

his hand so shaky holding the spoon,
then he jerked and pulled away
as she touched his foot under the table
to say she loved him and things were OK,

PERVERT

but he jumped and pulled away,
with his face just like her own crushed,
though she would always be OK with him
wanting to explore his other side where

DON'T TOUCH HIM

his face just like her own could flush
with heat not shame, that same
desire to uncover his other side running
through his coding, unstoppable,

PERVERT

and one day heat would override shame,
although neither of them knew that then,
because his coding, unbreakable,
would find a way to come out

PERVERT

but neither of them knew that then,
with their father's word in red
blocking his one way to come out,
standing on the table between them,

PERVERT

their daddy's capital word in red
branding him the worst kind of child
standing on the table between them, and
they must eat his word before getting down,

PERVERT

her brother branded the worst ever child.
Afterwards, she would always remember
having to eat his word before getting down,
that taste of cardboard for breakfast.

DON'T TOUCH HIM

The bottle

Childless aunt, her opinion didn't count:
she couldn't know what it took to raise
a child. It was daddy who knew best,
and it was best for baby that her mother's breast
was subbed for the bottle so he could do his bit.

She saw her sister hide her aching tits
behind a rictus of veneers, the pregnancy plump
shearing to sharp angles, her glow fading like
Tinkerbell's star. Kept at four counties' length,
she caught the birthday/Christmas snippets but

little else. That first feed stayed with her for years
though, her niece's red and bawling stress, eyes
scrunched so wet and fists punching as daddy
rammed the bottle home, saying that she had to take
it and he knew what she needed, that this teary

mess of sound and milk would quieten, she would
be glad to drink his wisdom, should suck it and be
grateful. Childless aunt, her opinion didn't count
at eighteen when her niece asked questions so much
like her aunt that the influence was branded

a contagion. She needed top-ups from the bottle,
or there could be no cure: how dare they chew the teat,
spitting it from their mouths? How dare they rinse him
out when that white trickle should have been enough?

Narcissus to his mirror

Come over here, pretty boy, and let's look
at you. It's been a while. Don't forget I
knew you when you were *Narcissus*, not trendy
Narc, when you were fixated on me, not shy
to check your crowsfeet in my depths. Mummy's
boy you were then, always begging her to cover me
with a towel. I couldn't work out if you were afraid
your gorgeousness in my glass would age, or if we
were lying to each other, neither you nor I anything
like we seemed. But now, here we are – me a bit
cracked at the corners and you - well, cracking up
is probably the kindest way to phrase. You're shitty
to your mum, you know. Forget what you look like
for a moment – silverfox suits you anyhow. Her smile
wobbles at the corners, eyes fixed on nothing, miles away.
Proud now? Yes, she's worried ill about you, those are all
her pills on the cabinet shelf. Go on, take some – the small
blue ones will do it. I know you need *my* help, to help yourself.

Why I like metal detecting

First job was at sea, then after the war I went
working underground. Bad luck, to have been
hit and sunk, then watch my mates buried alive
after that pit shaft collapsed. Now I can't unsee

both things. Nights are worst, when the lads come
crying out, burning, flesh smoking as I pull them free,
but there's always more behind, their faces blanked
with dust, coughing my name as they scream.

I don't work anymore. This is just a hobby, pain
in my back and knees stops me doing too much
and the voices never leave. I know when I die
I'll see them properly, be able to reach and touch

their faces which won't be black or charred. But for
now, I listen to the earth; I like to hear her scars.

On top of the mountain, 1956

I love the way you listen to each other
on the phone, keep that hidden speaker on
so you can always hear what I or my brothers
call to ask; how tired you are, how well you slept.

Your face is pink and shiny in the mist, windswept
curls a damp dark tangle on his shoulder, the new
unblemished ring rests lightly on his knee. It crept
up on you, you said; his shy charm, that long tall stride

you still kept pace with right until this year. You cried
out in your sleep again last night, he said. Now I see
how this will go, how one of you will disappear inside
like cloud on top of the mountain. The one left

behind will replay these voices, dust the frame, and
nothing will prepare us for this, the sight of them bereft.

Letters from Libya

RAF El Adem, 1960

My darling, we are miles south of the sea,
our camp a bleached canvas reef against
storms of sand so wild, the locusts that we
loathe seem like a blessing after. Our tents

are all we have in this strange place to keep
us anchored. The fruit cake that you sent
stays cool above my bed; it welcomes sleep
with each moist crumb. The warm spice scent

of brandy wafts me home – your soft, sweet
face, tumble of dark curls, hot hand in mine.
And Nina and Frederik sing to stoke this heat:
'Listen to the Ocean' beats its rhythmic line.

The desert blooms in winter, darling, when
it rains. I climb the aerial tower at night
to count the stars and bullet holes, then
watch brave flowers close in fading light.

Did I write about the frog, darling? Outside
the hall first thing each day, he sits in a tiny
pool under the dripping tap. The harsh tidal
sun soon scorches it away, his bright shiny

form vanished like the shade till evening falls.
They called this place The End, darling, and I
fear it when the mines explode as we install
the cables, brown plumes erupting to the sky.

X XXXX XXX

Postcards from Powys

Aberangell, 1966

The baby is so good, Mum, she wakes
up once at night but never cries, makes
me feel bad that I cry all the time, lie
here soft with tears, racking my mistakes.

We walked eight miles today, Mum, and took
the baby with us; that old map book
showed Gwastadcoed, a farm we'd spotted from
the road. No harm done to take a look.

Mum, I can't wait to leave this dark place.
The owner's sadness stains her sharp face
although she's kind to baby, and to me.
She doesn't mind her in this small space.

We packed our stuff last night Mum, and left
first thing this morning. The brown plump cleft
of Bracken Hill tugged at us round each bend.
He hugged me tight; said I looked bereft.

The farm is very quiet, I hear
all her little sighs. I feel the fear
spike but try not to let it take me, Mum.
You'd like the view. I wish you were here.

Songs of Saudi

I. SHONA'S SONG

Morpeth, September 1990

When war comes, nobody knows how
long it will last and we left so fast,
our lovely life a blur in the taxi
mirror, a trail behind the plane

dial tone

which didn't last and we left so fast,
there was no time to ask you to look in the
mirror, to follow our trail behind the plane
and track us here to these cool grey days

ring tone

there was no time to look, you wouldn't ask
with war one more work decision
and the track to our cool grey days
already cold and failing in the Western light.

dial tone

This war was one more work decision
in the walk of life, warm Eastern spice
an already fading taste in Western nights,
but the mums are all so kind here

ring tone

in our new way of life, warm Eastern spice
delights them in the voices of our boys
and the mums are kind to us here, my nightly
terror of the phone high out of reach

dial tone

hidden by the voices of our boys,
their golden smiles keep
the panic of the phone out of my reach,
and terror is a weapon in war

busy line

their smiles golden with sleep
while I sweat the distance, hear the hum
of terror in those sleek weapons
that fly across our screen and yours

dial tone

and I sweat and hum, hear you already
holding the phone tight to make it ring
while they fly across our screen and yours
so far away, with you in our safe house

ring tone

clutching the phone to make it ring,
our children singing on the roof seems
far away now, when we were safe in our house
with every day sunny, every day blue sky

dial tone

with children singing on the roof. It seems
our life was lost like luggage in the taxi
along with every sunny day, every blue sky.
War came, and nobody knows when it will end.

empty line

II. SUHEIL'S SONG

Dhahran, October 1990

I am the man in the bathtub, calling you
from my ivory tank, a stubborn fish
stuck in a pond without water to protect
against gas and bomb, only a mirror to

busy line

reflect this solid tank, a stranded fish
in this rich place, no lack of anything,
even gas and bomb, only a mirror to
see me talking, although missing you

dial tone

in a rich place with no lack of anything
is not the point. The mirror wall
shows me talking, and missing you
so far away shows we're tied together

ring tone

but that's not the point. The mirror wall
makes everything bigger than it is,
you so far away and us not together,
but separation builds deeper ties,

ring tone

makes everything bigger than it is,
the sky truth blue, the sand heart gold,
and separation ties us deeper, builds us up
while the sun sulks red each night

empty line

my truth sky blue, my heart sand gold,
and their tiny half-heard voices make
my face wet red each night
without a bedtime story

ring tone

and their tinny half-lost voices make
home a question, here in the safe house
without my bedtime story
that home is family is home,

ring tone

without family here in the safe house
with taped windows and CNN,
as my family makes home without me
and the heat reeks through the aircon,

busy line

licks the taped windows, and CNN keeps
those fighters coming in my dreams.
The heat seeps through the aircon
but your cool voice in my right ear

dial tone

says fighters are nothing but dreams,
and the pond without water will defend
and you are my voice, my right, my dear one,
and I am the man in the bathtub, calling you.

ring tone

III. OMAR AND IMRAN'S SONG

London, May 2017

"Our voices sound so much the same, I can't tell which of us is speaking."

Dear brother

Our lunch today was such a treat, to meet you and the little one, voices from other tables fading into background while the warm sound of our past filled space between salt and ketchup. You've been gone so long around the world I'd forgotten how big things were when we were small, how much we shared during the war when we were both the Evac Kids, different in the way we spoke and looked, the way we laughed at clouds and rain, the very same response to sunshine on our skin, that hazy beat of home. I worry how to begin. I can't be the same as you about the way ahead; I forget the many things I have to do, can't remember which bit of the future I've agreed to follow. I need you, brother. Please tell me how to live today and play it forward, stop staring at the years behind which muddle up my mind and keep me tethered to that geek in glasses, the tease of teenage taunts which scar. I loved seeing you today, brother; just us swapping stories of blue-sky-yellow-sun; how *Dad* and *Mum* is once again *Baba* and *Mama* and we're forever safe in Saudi heat speaking low, and giggling in the air-conditioned hum.

Dear brother

Speaking to you today hooked me straight back to nappy days; my thumb is aching to be sucked, that special comfort lost for twenty years. Both of us seemed to be in tune, brother; we were happy to give some of ourselves, to share our views of home, the one true space which we agree is where you should rest easy, place your flag. When I tell you tales of travel, my adventures in the sun, I know we can't go back to when the heat felt like a sister, why I keep moving forward without pause. The day we left I cried the same small tears that you did, I lied about it all, that weird grief the thing to hold chest-tight like a stuffed bear. Even now I feel the shame too much, my hot wet trousers shrieking loss as my name made me a thief, so I changed it, swapped it over with the other to find myself again. There is no sound better than little ones laughing, brother. My boy today reminded me of when our voices changed from threats to something golden, the kitchen knife held to your eye our terrible secret switched by magic into joy, your smile had all that power.

Three-ply

I. YOUNGEST

He smiles slyways at the camera
while you scud down the slope
to the river, his sticky hidden palm
a firm shove print on your back. I hope

you landed softly, didn't cry your fears
of cows and calves staking claim
to sunpatch heaven, stayed still
waterside till he teased your name.

Then he made you scramble, those
elasticated jeans dragging pats
up the bank in their frayed hems,
brown trails scouring his nose.

You are the dropped stitch, the third thread,
the selvedge child, the carriage head.

II. MIDDLE

While he battles with a rock so big
his pudgy fists barely span,
you deadeye Dad's camera, can

feel your lips twitch a grin
at the flat skimmer you hold up in
proof of skill and judgement.

You are the cross stitch, the double rib,
the wool loop child, the grafting sib.

He will make a noisy splash, but
you will launch the longest throw, no
wet feet for you. Your stone will go

on and on; stun the other bank with a thud,
make those dozing cows choke their cud,
wake us to your aim, your absolute certainty.

III. OLDEST

I am the lockstitch, the first strand,
the fully-fashioned child, the weft by hand.

Neither of you saw me watching. Dad
didn't pan me into shot, shadowed
in the window behind the curtain, had
never thought to get the sentinel child
in on this pastoral act. You two showed
how boys could be boys, dynamic duo
trekking through the grass like geese who
head for home after hissing off strangers.

But you knew where I would be. You were aware.
The camera couldn't catch your faces but I
frame them as I see them now. And if I dare
my wish, when I least deserve it you're both there.

St Margaret's and the farmhouse

We were never friends, you and I;
your people slavish to the soil, my
people obedient, for the most part,
to the cross. The two only met at mart,

some half-hearth, others strictly Book
not crook. And mine never took
yours seriously, not until they
raided my foundations, paid way

over the evens to that wily clerk
who flagged stones strong enough
to build your central stack. Rough
hewn? Well, yes – we both are. Dark

Red Mansfield blocks keep us propped
down the ages. Proof that God just
might have some joint plan for us,
perhaps; an end left open, unstopped,

where we still face each other east to west,
salute our long endurance, pass His test.

The Will of John Barton of Holme by Newark

10th December 1490

I am tired now, not just of age and sickness but of the
constant quarrels here in my house at Holme. My sheep
shout across cold fields tonight; I hope the Thomases have
reckoned to give them the good hay for which I paid
much this last harvest, they must make best weights for
lambing and keep full fleeces, all.

Isobel says I care more for the sheep than her and all
our children together. Tonight I will put this right, but the
two older boys fight as they always have, and my sheep
are calm and good and certain – they have
never let me down. Since I first bought and paid
for four strong ewes, a young farmer with nothing for

myself except an eye for fine wool and appetite for
something more than fields, they have been all
and everything for my fortune. When the
men around bickered and dealt me low, sheep
were my passage across the sea – their fleeces have
built these walls, lined my wife's best cloak, paid

for everything my boys crave and covet. They say I paid
for my family with the staple, as if I should be ashamed for
that, but while my body falters in this bed like an ailing tup, all
my thoughts are as proud and strong as my best ram, him the
animal I leave to the church for mortuary and my soul. Sheep
would agree together as my heirs cannot, would have

the sense to be content and quiet around a dying man – they have
a dignity I could not buy, and my boys will not earn. Debts paid
by their wool are honestly waged, something to be thankful for
in these ungracious days when what remains of my work is all
the items here on this parchment. They will wear my coats in the
days to come, stroking my mink and velvet while denying the sheep

their part, pretend their father merchanted anything but sheep,
as if cordwainers and vintners were a cut above. They have
much to learn, my querulous flock. They think I have paid
the notary to write this out tonight on a whim, but they take me for
a lesser man if they believe I would leave them this house and all
my chattels without condition. First they must agree, or the

whole subdivides into smaller parts. Heaven lies
in the detail, and while I thank God, and always shall,
the sheep have paid for all. My will be done.

Dame Elizabeth Broughton answers the court

15th April 1727

Sir, I am entirely a stranger to proceedings here.
You must forgive a poor widow's lack of grasp,
for in all such matters prior, my dear late husband
Sir Brian Broughton would stand. Since his demise

all must forgive my widow's grasp, my lack of
certainty. I have not slept, the thought of how
Sir Brian would not stand for this and his demise
weighs heavy on my mind, for I am growing more

certain, despite not sleeping, that the thought of
Anne Carter and her claims for full annuity would
weigh too heavy on his mind, of this I am more sure.
She was a scandal and a scold, beg pardon the court,

the name Anne Carter and her canny claims would
have ruined a lesser man, but not my husband.
He pardoned her the scandal, I begged and scolded
him to end his visits to her, but he courted disaster

like a lesser man, was briefly not at all my husband.
Those boys she had, he hoped them his, would only
end his visits when he saw William Hodgson courted
her, how quickly she came undone, how hot she flushed.

Those boys she had were never his, his only hope of
siring heirs lost years before when his horse tipped him,
but the way she flushed and came undone, the heat
of her convinced him for a time that he had it in him

to sire heirs. I lost our boy when his horse tipped him
and they told me he was crushed, unlike to live.
He convinced me for a time he still had it in him
to recover, do his duty for the parish, but I knew

our hopes were crushed even as I learned to live.
Sir, I wander and you are right to rally me to task.
I am recovered, will state my duty for the parish but
I will not cede on the amount. Her boys have no right

to wander into our affairs and rally your support.
When Mistress Carter died in last year's fire, her
boys amounted to naught and I will not cede my rights.
What, sir, the fire? I know naught of how it started.

Anne Carter died and that's all I knew of it last year.
In such matters, my late husband would know best.
I had no part in that fire. May the court forgive me
for I feel entirely strange, sir. Proceed without me here.

Lord Byron to his mirror

*on the evening of 26th February 1812, the night before his maiden
speech to the House of Lords on the Frame-Work Bill*

Let me tell you this, my Lords: you may perceive
I am a man who will not abide injustice, the distress
of families broken like my county's frames. I believe
that hungry sons and daughters applied insufferable duress
to fathers pushed to be unworthy of their hire. It would relieve
us to rescind the capital of their crimes, show some little kindness...

...now then, that will do it; my tone should silence all the wary.
No one will guess I spoke for rioters because Captain Jack stole Mary.

No particular saint

Augustus William Lumley-Savile 1829-1887

Your Majesty, I have been but a silly man
of fashion, with a light touch in the cotillion
yet not much more of grace to tell. If I can
be redeemed by just one thing, it is to die

quietly here, in this bed that is not my own,
not one jot disrupted that my Villa Edelweiss
is now at your disposal, Ma'am. The throne
has been my joy to serve; all parties, jewels,

quick women nothing to me now I near
my end. I wish – ah, I wish for one more
tiny thing, if Your Majesty might hear
the last plea of a sinner and grant him

favour. You gift me these engravings which
are such a wonder; to share your likeness
and Her Royal Highness in profile is rich
beyond all imagining. But I would gladly

trade these peerless treasures for a stone
wreath in the small red church in Bilsthorpe
where I shall be interred, silent and alone.
My appetites have been the ending of me,

and Your Majesty has been kind to blink
a blind eye to my failings. My brothers
have despaired of my excesses, but I think
though I have been no *particular* saint,

I warrant lasting proof of my devotion,
want all to know my passion for my ruler,
strong in death. I beseech you with emotion,
Majesty, grant me hope with my last breath.

PART THREE

A hex for modern times

After his wife left him

Betrayal did that to the man,
clipped his heart and tipped
his wings with rocket fuel,
set him flying higher, harder,
faster, up and up till all he saw
was everything he could have,
everything he should have,
the world laid out in bite-sized
chunks, the rest shrunk to
pinheads, so tiny, crushable.

And there were two of her

although hardly anyone realised. The bigger
one was soft, had curly edges, smelled
like cake and jam, sprayed laughter in figures
of eight around the room to fold you in hugs
so close you could scarcely breathe, her lips
against your cheek gentle feathers of a love
confessional. You courted her ready quips,
applauded long lines late at night, those XXXs

at the end signifying nothing. The smaller
one snapped like peanut brittle, couldn't
pare the truth apart, a sharp-eyed crawler
craving everything you had: the larger slice,
a nicer chair. Her tiny claws snatched the rug
from under, socks too shiny to stop your fall.

Far gone

Not the desecration of a holy place, not the disrespect
to the slumbering dead, not the clichéd clinching as
ultimate titillator, the FU for your parents with their
preachy pouts and tutting brows. None of it shocked
me, I wouldn't have batted an uncaked lash if you'd
shagged all night, came back in the morning with
'*Loving Wife 1842-1879*' pressed into your dimpled
arse. What made me heave was your gleeful telling
of how far he'd gone, eyes glistening to match your
chin all scuffed and smeared, breath reeking of fish.

I wouldn't want to live there

Despite its open rural aspect, don't you
realise that local walking dogs gawp at
your coach-wide windows, peep in at night
as your teenage daughter flaunts in shorts
and vest across your heated flags, lit from
behind by roaring logs, flames fanning
unneighbourlies in the damp zip of their
waterproof trousers? It's not the mutts you
need to watch with your chickens, not *their*
jaws drooling, hawthorn pricked to crotch.

The angry man

It didn't take much to set him off – a question
turned back to face him, perhaps, its tail wagging
like one of his dogs who never walked to heel.
Up he went, inflated by injustice, face as red
as all those tomatoes broiling in his greenhouse,
finger wagging time to each snorted breath out,
spittle flying right and left from frothing jowls.
We learned vernacular from him, how the village
saw incomers, how some paths would never be
diverted, when to smile and wait for payback.

Too much always

Because they told him it was bad, too much always
seemed too good to miss. The fat boy never felt
thin inside, convinced himself that wobbly was the state to
be, patented excuses to dodge the burn. In his defence,
both parents had their issues, waistlines last seen in their
twenties heading south with chips and booze, rolled round their
ankles like trousers in the act. His jawline disappeared when
he was twelve, his neck at fifteen. He never saw
his willy without a mirror, stopped looking for it at
eighteen, told his dogs that God loved no matter what.

They go the opposite way

when they see her coming, hips and lips stretched
wide in false welcome, lies about this person and that
dripping from the dirty hole in her round, waxed face.
If they're not quick, they're pinned like Catherine wheels
to her red brick wall, doomed to whizz themselves silly
trying to escape, ears bleeding all the while with hot, sour
secrets poured and stoppered. Their only fault polite
hesitation when it mattered, their flaw spotted like a fox
sees the gap in roof planks, rips them up using her teeth,
tears heads off without a thought, strewing feathers.

Disgraceful

Feather boa, sequins, diamonds and lace,
Nut-brown bare arms and firm upright chassis –
so few wrinkles on that beaming face,
at 73, I want to be Shirley Bassey.

No bond can contain her, the dame is forever.
Feisty, fearless, well-sussed and sassy –
she may be a spender, spendthrift never never;
at 73, I have to be Shirley Bassey.

Belting voice, smutty laugh, star-spangled life,
diva supreme from a Tiger Bay lassie.
OK, not every man's ideal wife,
but at 73, I must be Shirley Bassey.

Thigh slits, stilettos and festival wellies –
no wheelchair for me, I'll stay wiggle my assy.
Tight-fitting gowns will restrain all my bellies
and at 73, I will be Shirley Bassey.

Stick or twist

I've got the scent of something new
but not sure what I ought to do.
Chance to seize, or to be missed?
Is it time to stick or twist?

My natural instinct's just to do it,
I rarely ever doubt or rue it.
It's not like me not to persist
but is it time to stick, or twist?

There's lots of merit in this notion
and risk diminishes with motion...
perhaps I ought to make a list?
It might be time to stick – or twist?

Something's bound to tip the scales
to keep me off, or on, the rails.
I'll shut my eyes and call the trick.
I think it's time to twist. Or stick?

Success

The unfurled tongue of his ambition
tripped him up at every turn.
It didn't match his shirt or socks
just like a tie would,
and he couldn't ever seem to learn
to keep it tucked away
inside his pinstripes of performance,
safe from colleagues' narked and sharpened eyes.
The luring ladder of advancement always
blew caution off in favour of the prize.
So the steaming heap of peer resentment
grew warmer daily, fuelled the fire.
Oblivious to all around him,
he sailed on past his self-made pyre
(next to the copier, fax and cooler,
around the corner from Accounts).
Cubicle innuendo stoked it hourly,
in neatly measured,
flammable amounts.
Blinkered, he failed to spot the obvious:
no one liked him,
no one cared,
no one offered him a coffee,
holiday toffees never shared.
Promotion all that mattered to him,
the praise of corridors above his head
made him stone to those around him –
all his staff who wished him dead.

A hex for modern times

Don't worry about all the arcane stuff you
used to have to gather from obscure places.
There's none of this frog's bane, moondew,
bloodspore nonsense now. All ancient traces

of our beliefs are banished like deleted files,
you won't find twigs or bones or funny
coloured dust that tastes like devil's bile
in the backs of our cupboards. The honey

really will be honey, not some vile sap
stolen from a tree with a name no one will
pronounce. No, all you need today is a lap
top, a printer and a basic knowledge, then fill

in the gaps with Google, a good name for our great
witch if ever there was one. And then you print
their email – it doesn't matter which but latest
is best to preserve the aura. Top tip, don't stint

on ink as we need strong black marks
to do thing properly. Smooth the sheet, feel
their words rise and fight, your fingers dark
with drying carbon connected to the earth, real

power building as you rub the weary serifs
of their name, wish them every way to hell,
or worse. And that's it, the simple starter spell,
a hex for modern times. Think of yourself as sheriff,

not necromancer. Without us, there'd be no lore
in this online town, no justice in an unseen war.

The meeting

At the meeting to twist our fate,
the blue man's fingers stretch out straight
and beckon us into his lair.
I trot on in with perky hair
and do my best to concentrate,

not laugh too loud when through the gate,
or with reception remonstrate.
Ignore their snubs, time to beware –
                    at the meeting.

Black seats line up to demarcate
the battle plan of our debate.
Strategically I choose my chair,
and sit to face the name-matched pair
who share no other single trait,
                    at the meeting.

While blue eyes beg, brown alienate,
stay looking down while lips set bait
to trap us in a spreadsheet snare,
                    at the meeting.

Sweat stains seep through and decimate
the calm one tries to cultivate,
betrayed by glands and tight fit wear,
still no response, no upward stare.
I wish my heels could mutilate,
                    at the meeting.

I ply some charm, to arbitrate
but mortar shells reverberate
around the room, tempt me to swear
and start to lose the will to care –
but suddenly, we're done. Checkmate.
                    End of meeting.

The mice at The Troubadour

When the last poet has stanzaed up
the stairs, the mice at The Troubadour
shimmy down the dark brown curtain,
gather up crisp crumbs and stray peanuts,
and form a whiskery horseshoe round the stage.
Without the spotlight, it's hard to see who's showed up
for tonight's critical review, but the ritual opening chant
of *'We will read it, we will heed it, we will make it new, new, new'*
(inspired by too many daytime reruns of Bagpuss) fills
the empty basement with a sweet high rhythm. Tails flick
back and forth in the gloom, dust and peanuts agitated
in equal measure as Beardy Mouse kicks off
with a faultless rendition of the guest poet's latest oeuvre.
Titter Mouse starts to giggle, rocking in time to the heavily emphasised end
beat of alternate lines, surprising herself with a full head-over-tail tumble
at the finish. All agree it is Beardy's – and the poet's – finest to date,
but no one will buy the book. Next up, Diva Mouse debates the wisdom
of audience participation in phonetic verse, particularly under the cosh
of a timed slot. It's 50/50 for and against. When all the engaged
squeaking subsides, Northern Mouse pitches some hard vowels
into the silence to spice things up. He reminds everyone
that it might be grim past Watford Gap, but peanuts
are bigger, cheaper, and available in a wider range
of flavours. And things are just getting going, and
Uppity Mouse has run up a chair leg
in indignation for the first time that night,
when the heavyweight paw of Muldoon smacks
through the catflap at the back of the cellar,
skittling beer bottles like a caesura.
A surge of grey and brown skates
back up the curtain, along hanging
wires and the safety of joists and
beams, with the smart-arse echo
of *'We'll alliterate, articulate,*
accelerate, we're much smarter
and faster than you' hanging like
enjambment in the air.

Cobbler Bob

I'll tell you the story of Cobbler Bob,
or as much as my Dad says he knows:
shoes were his life and shoes were his job,
and it's from him I get my big nose.

Bob had a shop in old Arnold town,
Dad says it was probably on Front Street:
not far from our office, a few doorways down,
a place to look after the folks' feet.

Bob was Dad's granddad, an angry old man
who'd survived fighting in the Great War.
Mamma, his daughter, went to live with her gran
when he yelled at her mum *cheating whore*.

Bob brought back a Luger as a war souvenir
as well as his jealous obsessions.
He'd sit up all night in his shed without fear,
primed to shoot, save his precious possessions.

Bob's son chucked the gun into old Bestwood Lake
which is where it remains to this day.
Bob channelled his rage and managed to make
his shoes worth the top rate of pay.

Bob's soles were the toast of the toffs of the Shire,
detailed patterns with expert fine stitching.
Mamma stayed with gran and avoided his ire,
learned all about séance, and witching.

Bob is long gone now but his soles remain
in a local displaycased museum.
Dad thinks that he knows where to find it again,
if ever I wanted to see them.

So I've told you the story of Cobbler Bob,
or as much as my Dad claims he knows:
shoes were his life and shoes were his job,
and I'm glad all I got was his nose.

Rejoice

Let bells ring out, we've been invited
to yet another wedding this year.
We can't refuse, they'd feel so slighted,
we've got to go, the church so near.
I try my best to look enchanted
at big meringue, the bride's tattoo.
The choir has wailed, the vicar's ranted
and confetti's chucked – now to the 'do'.
It's alright for you, best bib and tucker,
the aunties' favourite, always kissed.
You leave me while you shake and pucker –
your little closet atheist.
Quick note to self: just smile and fake it.
Hush that voice hissing *they won't make it*.

My time

The water's there but I won't drink.
Leave me alone, I need to think.
Ignoring you is not a crime –
I won't be pushed, I'll take my time.

What you've said makes lots of sense –
just wait a while, take no offence.
I understand the paradigm,
but won't be rushed, I'll take my time.

The more you speak, the worse I get.
My heels dig in, I get upset,
my ears heal up, your talk is mime –
I won't be hushed, I'll take my time.

You may be absolutely right,
but banging on will cause a fight.
Don't rile a woman in her prime –
I can't be pushed. I'll take my time.

Paean

Twinging, cringing, swingeing, whinging,
throbbing, bobbing, gobbing, sobbing,
sighing, crying, lying, dying,
stretching, fetching, kvetching, retching,
heated, treated, standing, seated,
rolling, lolling, pole-axed, hollering,
curled up, flat out, cat arch, tea spout,
hanging, dangling, flopping, wrangling,
wet flannel, bathmat, cold tiles, bath panel,
ibuprofen, paracetamol, codeine, cocodamol
pressure points, panics, pins and needles,
begging, pleading, whimpers, wheedles,
dark room, blankets, pillows, wheat pack,
neck, head, elbow, knee, hip, lower back,
frozen peas, ice cubes, splashed with water,
dialling, desperate, mummy, daughter,
knackered, crackered, screwed up, steaming,
doped up, roped up, spaced out. Dreaming.

Kisses of time

Not kisses – well, not gentle, middle-aged 'good night dear are you still reading' pecks at any rate. More like full on, suck-your-face-off, deep throat with tongue and spittle snogs, with a few love bites thrown in for good measure in places you don't want people to see, the ones that don't fade quickly to green but stay black for ages. And if it's a snog, then it's with someone who doesn't pretend to love you, just wants to get in your large lady pants and come on hot and heavy, skip any light fingering that might make it bearable. Someone with halitosis, and sharp teeth scraping your lips, grey stubble snarking your chin and smelling faintly of bacon. Now you mention it, I don't think kisses are right at all. More like punches – 'the close-fisted, knuckleduster, sucker-punches of time' – that sounds about right.

The last LAFT

It's more than a little bit funny
(thank you, Elton) to find that,
after all this time and all my money,
the problem turns out to be what
no one could have actually seen: a short-
coming in every sense, a veritable taut
fusion of deficiency so deliciously ironic
that, had my pain not been this chronic,
I would have laughed loudly and so
long that my other abnormality might
contrarily correct itself, it being no
mean feat to stay stiff necked and right-
eous with a pelvis turned to stone,
each twist provoking the wrong type of groan.

5.15

So now I strip for you, sometimes twice
a week if I need you and you're free. I worry
that you'll spot the same black frill, low price,

high rise pants each time, in too much hurry
to plan a different pair to spice things up.
I feel your breath behind, smell faint curry,

cheesy onion crisps from lunch, coffee cup
still cooling on the side, the chewy mint
you swallowed before I came. Abruptly

you shift focus and it slides in. A hint
of sweat half cloaked by sandalwood hits
my nose, can't help but lift my head, squint

at the clock. You tug lace back to where it sits.
Magic. Pain gone. And there are other benefits.

Breakfast can wait

i.m. Prince Rogers Nelson 1958-2016

Oh baby, I wanna be your lover, but by the time you've heard my list of demands, I wonder if you'll wanna be mine. Yes, I'm the lubricated lady – I come with conditions attached:

1. <u>No diamonds and pearls</u>. I don't need a scarlet pussy to get off – those things chafe. If I'm going to get some solo, do the dance of desperation, then all I do is dream of my drawers burnin', think of a good dick and a job is done – soft and wet, breathless, broken. Bump this baby, then do it again.

2. <u>No bedtime roses, but a bedtime story never goes amiss</u>. We'll have big fun in that big brass bed with the big pump set to automatic, face down, false alarm – I'll feel u up, feel that friction from the lotus to the electric chair. Friend, lover, sister, do me again.

3. <u>All day, all night, baby, baby, baby</u>. All this love from an honest man means breakfast can wait. I'm your cinnamon girl, your chocolate, your cherry cherry, cold coffee and cocaine motherwife. Cream, get on top. Cream, shaboogy, bop. Count the days, cross the line, do me baby then do it again.

4. <u>Get it up, get off, hide the bone and hold me</u>. If you're a horny pony my blood is thicker than time, my bloody mouth bites the beat with your blue boy but you'd better call my name. Cause and effect counts the days, a dirty mind makes an empty room. Do me baby, but I'm extraordinary – don't play me, do me again.

5. <u>Be my mirror</u>. This curious child wants days of wild, delicious clouds so easy does it, boyfriend. For you, for love, for this erotic city in hallucination rain, hump me baby, then do it again. Funk this, baby, and do me. Again.

Losing my virginity to Frankie Goes to Hollywood

Not actually to Frankie, you understand, but
to that rainhissing Relax beat while cheap struts
of the bottom bunk creaked and smacked
at the blue Anaglypta wall. He lacked
the knack and patience to show me how to come
that first time when *Don't Do It* seemed like some
insistent dare, his paintflecked fingers thick and sticky
with me, my frantic tongue rough and licky
with him, saltsweat rubber and the smell of his leather
jacket blurring with chips from his mam's kitchen, weather
outside cold and wet, it was November I think, and what I wanted more
than anything was to have it done, to finally be sore
from him, so all the fumbling on dustsheets in the back of his van
could stop. It didn't, of course. We carried on using paint cans
as props and even now the smell of thinner brings back the crusty
feel of dried gloss rasping my bum while he'd thrust
deep in time to Frankie on repeat, each time a little slicker
and each time a little quicker, while I learned how to stroke his balls
the way he liked them, and he learned nothing at all
about the way my nipples hardened at his breath against my ear,
and how it now took only seconds to bring me near
enough.

Notes

PART ONE: ROSEMARY THRIVES

Mazey ball

Twitter 27/09/2018, 07:06 Maude Frome (@frome_maude):

Witches cannot resist wool, & this Mazey Ball from The Museum of Witchcraft in #Cornwall is so filled. It was believed "no witch could cast an evil eye on the owner until she had counted every bit of wool in the house." Aberdeen Press & Journal, 17th Nov 1932.

The green wood sculptor at Gabriel's Wharf

Friedel Buecking works mainly with the chain saw. For thirty years he has made rocking pieces, sculpted furniture and carvings of animals, people and abstract shapes. His playscapes and monumental outdoor sculptures in oak for many sites in and around London have been commissioned by community initiatives, schools and local authorities. For more information: friedelbueckingwoodsculptor.co.uk

PART TWO: WITNESS

Postcards from Powys

This poem is written in the traditional Welsh form of a gwawdodyn. Robert Lee Brewer, August 5th 2013: "The gwawdodyn is a Welsh poetic form with a couple of variations. However, both versions are comprised of quatrains (four-line stanzas) that have a 9/9/10/9 syllable pattern and matching end rhymes on lines 1, 2 and 4. The variations are made in that third line. One version has an internal rhyme within the third line, so there's a rhyme somewhere within the third line with the end rhyme on the third line. The other has an internal rhyme within the third line that rhymes with an internal rhyme in the fourth line. In both cases, the rhyme starts somewhere in the middle of the third line and is a unique rhyme to the end rhyme in lines 1, 2 and 4."

Songs of Saudi

The Songs of Saudi sequence was developed in collaboration with composer Omar Shahryar, and was based on recorded interviews with his mother, father and brother about their evacuation from Saudi Arabia during the Gulf War of 1990. The first poem in the sequence 'Shona's Song' became the lyrics to a performance piece for the 2017 Leeds Lieder Festival, with music composed by Omar sung by mezzo-soprano Emily Hodkinson.

The Will of John Barton of Holme by Newark

John Barton, who rebuilt Holme Church near Newark, Nottingham-shire, rose from being a simple farmer to become a leading wool merchant and Mayor of the Staple of Calais. He died in 1491, leaving his wealth and chattels in a detailed will. It is apparent from the wording of the will that there was discord between his children (four sons, two daughters) and his wife. A self-made man, he built his fortune in the wool trade at a time when English wool was the most sought after in Europe, and there were around three sheep to every person. Bishop Hall of Norwich, the poet and satirist, observed in 1612: "There were wont to be reckoned three wonders of England, ecclesia, foemina, lana — churches, women and wool." It is said that the windows of John Barton's house in Holme carried the inscription: "I thank God, and ever shall. It is the sheepe hath payed for all."

Dame Elizabeth Broughton answers the court

Dame Elizabeth Broughton was the widow of Sir Brian Broughton who counted Bilsthorpe as part of his estate. On the 15th April 1727, she defended herself in court against a bill of complaint brought by William Hodgson. The gist of the matter appears to be that Sir Brian promised an annuity to his mistress Anne Carter, which Dame Elizabeth has defaulted on. During further research, it appears that Dame Elizabeth had been previously accused of causing the death of Anne Carter in a fire, and her relations are now retrospectively claiming the annuity as it was passed to them after her death. In transcripts of the court record, Dame Elizabeth defends herself vigorously, claiming that she is 'entirely a stranger' to all allegations and claims.

Lord Byron to his mirror

The Debate on the Frame-Work Bill, 27th February, 1812 was one of Byron's most famous public statements in support of the stocking frame-workers of Nottinghamshire. The frame-workers had been breaking up new machinery which was driving them into poverty and the militia were called out, led by Jack Musters, Byron's rival for the hand of Mary Chaworth. The Act before the House proposed increasing the penalty for frame-breaking from fourteen years' transportation to hanging. For more information: petercochran.files. wordpress.com/2009/03/house_of_lords_speeches.pdf

No particular saint

"Augustus Savile was the second natural son of John, eighth earl of Scarborough. For the first 54 years of his life he was known as Augustus Lumley and was poor but a man of great social influence and popularity. He then succeeded his elder brother in the property of Rufford Abbey, Nottinghamshire, the ancient seat of the Saviles, whereupon he took the name of Savile. However, his fortune came too late as he had very poor health and retired to die at his villa of Edelweiss near Cannes, unfortunately being disturbed by Queen Victoria in his final days as she moved into the villa as his guest. Augustus had to move out to die elsewhere. The Queen visited him on his deathbed and presented him with two signed engravings of herself and her daughter, which pleased him greatly, an example of 'the ruling passion strong in death' [Alexander Pope]. He died as he had lived, a courtier. He never married; and although no particular saint, his life was free from scandal." Thames Advertiser, 28th June 1887, page 3. He is buried in St Margaret's Church, Bilsthorpe, where an ornate monument, bearing a preserved wreath, carries an inscribed brass with the following inscription:

This wreath was sent by her Most Gracious Majesty
Queen Victoria
On the occasion of the Funeral at Bilsthorpe of the late
Augustus William Savile Esqre
Of Rufford Abbey, Ollerton, Notts.
her Majesty's Assistant Master of Ceremonies
who died at Cannes aged 58
on the 13th of April 1887.

Kisses of time

"Our bones and joints are not attractive when x-rayed, especially if we are a bit older ... X-ray findings do not necessarily match pain. Changes are likely to be age-related changes (the kisses of time)." Butler, D. S. & Moseley, G.L. (2010) Explain Pain, 7th ed. Adelaide: Noigroup Publications

The last LAFT

"Disc is an unfortunate name for the remarkable structures that intermarry vertebrae. They are not, at any stage of life, like discs ... We suggest that they should be called 'living adaptable force transducers' (LAFTs). (Which, incidentally, means that between the 5th lumbar vertebrae and the pelvis is the 'last LAFT')." Butler, D. S. & Moseley, G.L. (2010) Explain Pain, 7th ed. Adelaide: Noigroup Publications

Breakfast can wait

Prince was a prolific writer of songs for himself and others. The titles of around 90 of these songs (A-F) appear in this poem.

Acknowledgements

Some of these poems, or versions of them, have appeared elsewhere. Thanks are due to the following publications, publishers and competitions: Beautiful Dragons, Brittle Star, East Riding Festival of Words Competition 2018, Iron Press, Lighten Up Online, Live Canon 154, Magma, Marsden Village Together Competition, Mary Evans Poems & Pictures Library, Milestones Competition, Naugatuck River Review, Nottingham City of Literature, Places of Poetry, Poetry Business, Poetry Wales, Popshot, Shoestring Press, Skylark Review, Skylight 47, Stonewood Press, The Interpreter's House, The Nottinghamshire Historian, WOLF Competition, YorkMix Competition 2019.

Special thanks to Omar Shahryar and his family for their help with the 'Songs of Saudi' sequence, and to Nottinghamshire historian Jeremy Lodge for providing such rich material for the poem about John Barton of Holme.

I'm very grateful for the ongoing support and encouragement of Mahendra Solanki, Jacqueline Gabbitas and Martin Parker. And for Alan Slaney's love and tolerance, without which none of this would be possible.